To John Maggott,
who passed
away one month
before the release
of this story.

Miracle At The Tute

by Chuck Gaither

© 2021 Chuck Gaither
All Rights Reserved.
ISBN: 978-1-7366747-0-3

Cover photo by Harold Chatlosh of the Wabash Plain Dealer Newspaper

CONTENTS

Advance Praise — 6

Acknowledgments — 10

Introduction — 11

CHAPTER ONE — 13

CHAPTER TWO — 19

CHAPTER THREE — 23

CHAPTER FOUR — 29

CHAPTER FIVE — 35

CHAPTER SIX — 45

CHAPTER SEVEN — 53

CHAPTER EIGHT — 61

Advance Praise for
Miracle At the Tute

I met Coach Chuck Gaither the summer of 1970. Meeting him was a very encouraging experience. I walked away thinking, "He really cares about me." Knowing that I was ineligible to play football that school year, he allowed me to hang out and get to know the team. He even allowed me to observe practices and travel to away games alongside the current roster. Because of Coach Gaither's positive attitude and his kindness towards me, I was motivated to try out for the basketball team and run track and field the following year. Coach was not only my coach but has grown to be one of my closest friends for the last 51 years. Thank you, Coach, for always being there for me!

— **Elix Brewer**
1973 Mile Relay State Champion

Hometown sports have enriched the lives of young athletes for generations, myself included. While it's no secret that I was never a great athlete, my seventh-grade basketball experience would teach me important lessons about teamwork, leadership, and life. Chuck's story reminds me of the rare gift a great coach is to his students, their families, their communities, and beyond. His rare combination of gentleness and toughness allowed him to nurture kids with distinct disadvantages while also pushing them to achieve more than they thought was possible. He is a man of few words, yet through his story you clearly see how his walk does the talking for him. May this story inspire you to dig a little deeper and reach a little higher.

— **Bill Gaither**
Grammy-winning music industry trailblazer, music historian, songwriter, producer, mentor, husband, father, and grandfather

Miracle at the Tute is a heart warming true story about what can happen when people believe in something bigger then themselves! Chuck Gaither is an amazing example of the positive impact a coach can have on their student-athletes. I really enjoyed the book - it was an easy read!

— **Mickey Hosier**
Athletic Director at alma Mater,
Alexandria Monroe High School, where
he holds the all-time career record for
assists (777). Starting point guard for Ball
State University 2000 MAC Championship
and NCAA Tournament bid

Miracle at the Tute is a wonderful and inspirational story of what can happen when a coach believes in his athletes and the athletes believe in him. Chuck draws us into his story as he motivates and loves his players to reach their potential in athletics, and more importantly, in life.

— **Stan Daugherty**
Retired High School and
College Basketball Coach

Chuck Gaither became a great friend to me after we moved to Grant County in 1978. I started to referee high school basketball in the late 60s and worked a lot of his games. Chuck was the athletic director at White's Institute at the time and I had a front row seat to watch how he truly cared for each student. He strived to make their lives better than the environment they came from. Chuck was a great role model and blessing to all students and staff at White's Institute. I, too, am blessed to call him my friend.

— **Fred Hamilton**
Indiana sports jounalist

Chuck Gaither was a great fit at Whites. He was perfect for the young people that he coached and mentored. Whites is a "calling" and Chuck Gaither answered the call. His book "Miracle At the Tute" is his testament that hard work, good disciple and a loving heart can change lives.

— **Dave Martz**
Longtime member of the Grant County Sports Hall of Fame Board of Directors, former track coach at Southwood High School, former athletic director and coach at Eastbrook High School

Having been granted the privilege to read the manuscript for this book before its publication, I learned a lot about Chuck Gaither that I hadn't known. A colleague for more than 50 years, I knew he was a great coach, fantastic athletic director, super human being and just a fun guy to be around. I didn't know what an outstanding high school career he had or that he had such a temper. But Chuck has a heart of gold and that comes out in this book. He shares the mission of White's Institute and his role in it throughout the book. I would encourage any young person who is considering going into coaching to read this book. Coaching is not about winning. Coaching is about relationships. And that's where Chuck is at his best.

— **Roy Church**
Friend and former sports writer

Chuck Gaither's book tells of the most outstanding athletic event in the history of Wabash County, Indiana. Read how a high school star athlete coaches at a small school, faces many challenges, and competes for a state Championship. Truly inspiring.

— **Dick DuBois**
Former teacher and coach at Southwood High School. Father was principal at Whites Institute, responsible for hiring Chuck Gaither

Acknowledgments

Throughout my life I have been blessed with good people around me who have guided, helped, and loved me. This book is for all those people, and for everyone I had the privilege of coaching or helping in some way because of the support system I was blessed to have.

I couldn't possibly name everyone who participated in the story you're about to read, but I specifically want to express gratitude to my parents, Gordy Hoheimer, Jim Law. Thanks also to my wife, Becky, and daughter Brandi, who spent a lot of time helping me make this book a reality.

To the young men I coached at White's Institute, you made every day a pleasure. I am eternally grateful to have been part of your lives. It is not possible to mention all the athletes I had the privilege of coaching. Some are mentioned in this story and others are not, but I appreciate and remember each and every one of you.

To one special student, Jim Oprisek, a student at White's for four-and-a-half years who had a rough start, I know I was hard on you, but you became like a son to me. I'm so proud of you. When you came back to White's after graduation to be a houseparent for so many years, everyone knew that if we ever needed help, we wanted you in our foxhole.

Hats off to every student and cheerleader who cheered us on and supported us through all the wins and losses. And I can't possibly offer enough thanks to the school staff and support staff for all your help and encouragement over the years. You are outstanding people.

Introduction

Whenever I visit my hometown of Fairmount, Ind., I am treated as if I am the mayor. Everywhere I go, I run into someone who remembers my days as a high school athlete — always quick to recall the victories. In reality, those people are the very reason I experienced those victories. They are the ones who cheered me on, year after year, and coached me to do the right things in the right ways. They held up a standard that brought out the best in me.

Starting at home, with my parents, I had strong examples. They urged me to live with integrity in every aspect of life. I remember one particularly memorable conversation I had with them after I made my first varsity team as a high school freshman. Mom and Dad sat me down and gave me "the word," as I like to call it.

First, they told me how proud they were of me, then my mother asked, "Did the coach give you any rules?"

I shared with her the standards of conduct the coach said he expected.

"Good. Now, if you break one of them, the coach won't get to deal with you because we will first," my mother responded.

I knew she was telling the truth.

Out of my deep gratitude for everyone who helped shape me, I present this story of what is possible when people invest in young men and women, and give them opportunities to become the best they can be. The details and stories in this book reflect my recollection of events and people in the early 1970s. The dialogue has been recreated using a combination of memory and newspaper articles. May these events inspire you to dream big and keep believing in what is possible when we learn to work together.

CHAPTER ONE
The Early Years

Most great stories have simple beginnings filled with details that might seem mundane at first. This is how my story begins. A story of simple beginnings and everyday events went on to change the lives of some incredible students who, in turn, forever changed me.

My hometown of Fairmount, Ind., is a rural town surrounded by farmland. This little corner of the American Midwest is best known for the people who started there. Fairmount was the childhood hometown of a number of well-known people, including: actor James Dean; Garfield comic strip creator Jim Davis; former director of the National Hurricane Center Robert Sheets; CBS News's six-time Emmy Award-winner, Phil Jones; *Snake Pit* author, Mary Jane Ward; and Native American artist and art education pioneer, Olive Rush.

The small-town atmosphere of the 1950s offered a slow, steady, nurturing environment where I grew up believing I could do great things, too. I, along with one brother and four sisters, was raised in a home where we knew we were loved and were convinced we could accomplish anything we wanted in life.

In our family lineage, as far back as I can trace, everyone was either an athlete or a musician. I was an athlete. Athletics were always an important part of my life. In fact, I can't remember a single season of my childhood when my life didn't revolve around sports, partially because I had a natural ability and partially because I worked hard.

Throughout junior high and high school, I played football, basketball, baseball, and ran track. I had great coaches who encouraged me and challenged me. I understood that if I wanted to be the best, I had to work the hardest. So that's what I did.

One evening when I was a sophomore in high school, I heard a car stop at the end of the driveway. I was shooting hoops in our driveway after dark, as I often did, when I looked up to see my cousin leaning out of his car window.

"What are you doing?!" he called out.

The answer seemed obvious. I was practicing basketball. It never occurred to me that he would find it unusual to practice in the dark. Not long after that, my dad installed a light near the basketball hoop.

I played varsity for every sport Fairmount High School offered to high school boys and I lettered all four years of high school in football, basketball, and track. Our school had a baseball program for two years during high school and I lettered in baseball those two years, as well.

I continue, to this day, to look back at the advantages I had — a supportive family that believed in me, coaches who encouraged me to be the best athlete and person I could be, and great neighbors.

One such neighbor was Gordy Hoheimer. Gordy spent hours and hours with the kids on our block, teaching us not only how to *play* sports but how to *be* good sports. I would come to realize that having this kind of community behind me was an advantage not every kid has. I'm forever grateful for that privilege.

I earned the name "Poke" when I was a young kid. Whenever I played neighborhood sports, the older kids got frustrated with me when they realized I could outrun them. One day, one of older boys got upset and said, "You aren't that fast. In fact, you're just pokey." So all the kids started calling me Pokey. Eventually it was shortened to "Poke." Most guys had nicknames back then, and mine stuck with me throughout high school and beyond. I'm sure there are plenty of people in my community who wouldn't recognize me as Chuck, only as Poke.

My high school years brought about some exciting victories that attracted the attention of college scouts. I won't go into all the details of my high school sports career, but I will offer a few highlights to provide a glimpse of the experiences that would shape my life and my future in many ways.

In basketball, I scored 1,396 career points and became the leading scorer in Grant County twice during high school. During my junior year, I tallied 426 points for a 20.1 average and during my senior year, I scored 484 points for a 24.2 average. I was named to the Mississinewa Valley All-Conference team twice and became the league's top scorer.

In football, I scored more than 40 career touchdowns, led Grant County twice in scoring and rushing, and made first-team all-conference for two years.

As a shortstop for the Fairmount baseball team during my junior and senior years, I didn't make a single error and led the team in hitting and RBIs.

I had 42 first-place finishes in track, despite an abbreviated senior year due to injuries. I competed in long jump, relays, and sprints.

When it came time for me to start looking at colleges, I was approached by several schools who offered me full-ride scholarships. The basketball coach at Butler University, Tony Hinkle, asked to meet with me about playing basketball for Butler. During our meeting, he pulled out letters from people in my hometown who recommended that he recruit me. There were letters from coaches and teachers, even one teacher I had never met, trying to convince him to recruit me.

Taylor Hayes coached at Sweetser High School, one of our rival schools in the county, before accepting a head coach position at William Penn College in Iowa. He remained friends with my high school basketball coach, Ray Cox, and began talking to Ray about recruiting me to play for William Penn.

Ray told him I would likely never agree to attend an out-of-state college. He even offered for me to live with him and his wife if I would come and play for William Penn.

Legendary coach, Don Odle, from Taylor University, spent countless hours at our house trying to recruit me. All the scholarship offers were generous and flattering. However, during my senior year, I broke my left hand in the first football game of the season. Then, after playing with a cast on my hand throughout the season, I got speared in the back after the last play of the last football game of my senior year. That injury caused me ongoing pain throughout the basketball season that year and I couldn't seem to shake it. I wasn't sure how much more my body could take. I still struggle with pain from that injury to this day.

For years, my entire life had revolved around sports and my body had paid a high price. Besides, I was in love with a young lady named Becky, whom I had known since the seventh grade. We were high school sweethearts and I knew I wanted to marry her. I got a job at Dana Corporation, an automotive manufacturing plant in Marion, Ind., and made plans to settle down.

Becky and I were married in March of 1960, the year after we graduated high school. We were both still 18 years old on our wedding day; Becky turned 19 the following month, and I turned 19 that June. Although we were just kids, marrying Becky proved to be the best decision I ever made. We made our home in Fairmount near our families and I worked for Dana Corporation, which was about 20 minutes north of us.

Coach Hinga from Ball State University even talked to me after Becky and I were married to see if I might consider playing basketball for Ball State. He recalled that I had scored 38 points against an outstanding team from Dunkirk that went on win sectional. That, along with my academic record, would give me the opportunity to go to school tuition free. He even offered to help Becky find a job in Muncie.

I soon realized I didn't want to work in manufacturing for

the rest of my life. I decided to go back to school and chose Ball State which, was a 20-minute drive southeast from Fairmount.

For six years, I took morning classes at Ball State, then worked a full-time shift at Dana from 3 to 11 p.m.. Between classes and work, I would stop at home for lunch before driving to Marion. During those years, we also had two young daughters. Life was busy and happy.

In 1967, during my sophomore year of college, I got a phone call from my former high school principal, Roland Dubois. He asked if he and the superintendent at White's Institute, Robert Curless, could come to Fairmount and talk to me. Mr. Dubois was then serving as the principal at White's Institute. They wanted me to consider joining the staff at White's High School, to serve as a teacher and coach. They even offered to hire me on a state permit, until I could complete my course work and officially get my teaching license.

I didn't know much about White's. I thought it was a prison school or reformatory school, and it was a thirty-mile drive from my home. The time did not seem right to leave Fairmount. I thanked them for thinking of me but turned down the offer and stayed on the path I was on, attending classes in the morning and working a shift at Dana each evening. After six years of working and going to school, I graduated from Ball State University with a bachelor's degree in Secondary Education Physical Education and a minor in History.

CHAPTER TWO
The Tute

During the summer of 1970, after I graduated from Ball State, Mr. Dubois and Mr. Curless came calling again. They talked me into visiting the school and taking a tour, but before I ever set foot on the grounds, I had pretty much made up my mind that I would not be interested.

I would learn that White's Institute originally came into existence because of the vision of a Pennsylvania Quaker named Josiah White in the mid-1800s. He left money in his will to carry out his dream for a self-contained home where impoverished children could be educated and cared for, regardless of race or skin color.

In 1852, two years after his death, a six-hundred-forty-acre plot of land was purchased in north central Indiana, four miles south of Wabash, where White's Institute would be built. The school went on to become a home and school for orphans and wards of the court who came from Indiana, parts of Ohio, and Michigan.

Becky and I were invited to the campus for a visit, along with our girls, and as we drove onto the grounds, what we saw was nothing like I had imagined. The campus was an expansive quaint, countryside village with ponds, woods, and five hundred acres of farmland, complete with cows, pigs, and horses.

At the center of the campus were well-maintained buildings that housed the school, cafeteria, gym, office, store room, and bus barn. There were also amenities, including a pool, bowling alley, canteen, laundry facility, farm shop, lawn shop, and even a hospital.

Seven boys housing units, known as Divisions 1 through 7, were located at the north end of the property. Each unit was staffed by houseparents and assistant houseparents. Divisions 1 through 4 held younger boys; 5 through 7 housed older boys and contained a shared recreation room and kitchen.

Tidy brick homes lined the south end of the property, as well as apartments, and four girls housing units known as Divisions 8 through 11. The girls each had their own room, and the girls units also contained a shared recreation room and kitchen. Each was staffed by houseparents, a counselor, and assistant houseparents.

As we walked through the classrooms, cafeteria, gym, and student dorms, we were met by well-behaved students. There were no walls or fences, just students going through their daily activities, well-supervised by houseparents or staff members.

Every student was assigned a specific job on the campus, such as lawn maintenance, farming, cafeteria duties, laundry duties, lifeguards, or jobs in the storeroom or mechanic shop. Each week, half of the students attended classes while the other half worked their jobs. The following week, they switched. The school was in session year all year long, without summer breaks.

I was impressed with the facilities and the opportunities offered to students, many of whom had no family or community support. I couldn't imagine kids going through life without someone who believed in them, and the more I learned about White's, the more I began to see this opportunity in a new light.

As I walked around the picturesque campus with Becky and our girls, I felt an undeniable tug on my heart. This was a place I might be able to make a difference. We went home that day and weighed the decision carefully. We prayed a lot and talked it over with our families.

I asked for advice from my friend, Jim Law, who was one of

the best football coaches in Indiana and he told me it would be an extremely tough assignment, but he would support me all the way if I accepted the job. He had been my student teaching advisor at Oak Hill High School and was a highly respected teacher, so having his input meant the world to me.

After a week of back-and-forth discussions, Becky and I agreed that I couldn't turn down this opportunity. So, at 28 years old, I accepted the offer and became the physical education teacher, head football coach, head track coach, and assistant basketball coach at White's Institute.

We moved our family into a nice three-bedroom brick home on campus. As with all the school's staff housing, our utilities were all paid, and we received free groceries from the school's storeroom each week. We were also given free access to the cafeteria whenever we wanted. We felt incredibly blessed for those provisions.

Soon after settling in our new home, we got our girls enrolled in the local public school and it was time for me to get to work. I knew I had a big job ahead of me and was grateful for a strong wife who was willing and able to stand with me in the face of any challenge.

On my first morning at this new assignment, I walked briskly toward the gym to take inventory of the football equipment. Taking in the morning air as I made my way down the sidewalk, I met a female student who appeared to be fifteen or sixteen years old.

"You are the new football coach, aren't you?" she inquired.

"Yes," I replied as I turned to move on.

"Before I leave here, I'm going to f—k you," she replied.

I was in shock, then I thought maybe I'd misunderstood her.

"What did you say?" I retorted. She repeated herself, and she had said exactly what I thought I heard.

I immediately turned around, sped back to the house, and recounted the interaction to Becky. I told her I felt that I'd made a mistake and that maybe this job was not suited for me after all.

Becky sat me down and gently, lovingly reminded me that

these kids were at White's because they needed support and direction in life. They needed love, discipline, and guidance.

"You are *exactly* what these kids need," she insisted.

Perhaps that was the moment the reality sunk in that I would be more than a coach or a teacher at White's. Every one of the students needed a caring adult in their lives who saw their potential rather than their past. This school, which students affectionately named "the Tute," would prove to be the adventure of a lifetime.

CHAPTER THREE
Blood, Sweat, & Roosters

White's Institute was home to White's High School and was considered a public school inside a private institution. With only 135 students, our high school was by far the smallest of the three high schools that comprised the Metropolitan School District of Wabash County. The other two schools in the district were Northfield High School and Southwood High School. At the time, Indiana had a one-class system in all sports. Both our track team and football team would have to compete against the largest schools in the state. I did not have high expectations as our first season approached.

When the time came to meet the athletes before football season, 27 players showed up for our first meeting. We were about to embark on four weeks of conditioning before the first official football practice, so this meeting was an opportunity for me to lay out our goals and expectations for the upcoming season.

I didn't know what problems had brought these kids to White's, and I promised them I would only evaluate them based on what I saw. I would never look at their case histories and would only view them as young men. They knew the rules at White's better than I did, so I expected them to follow those standards without exception.

Only seven of those 27 students had played football the previous year. Eight others met my sight test. The rest of them did not seem to know anything about the sport. Most of the kids who attended White's had never played on an organized team before. I had my work cut out for me.

We began conditioning every day except Sundays. White's had very few weights, but Mr. Curless assured me he would get whatever I needed. He didn't have a set budget for the athletic department, but he said if I could justify an expense, he would sell some livestock or grain to raise funds as needed. So, the next week, hogs were sold and weights were on the way.

During the weeks that followed, I came to realize there were a handful of decent athletes. Most of the others I would not expect to contribute to the team in any way. Two sophomores in particular grabbed my attention: John Maggott and Mike McDonald. Just watching them run, I could see their smooth strides and knew they had a natural ability.

Most people called John Maggott "Big John" because of his size and athletic ability. He had come to White's from Cleveland, Ohio, when he was a junior high student. He had been in foster care after being taken away from his mother; he had never met his father.

Early on, I told Becky that I was pretty sure Big John didn't like me. She laughed and disagreed. She told me she had watched him hover closely in the background, listening to every word I was saying. I learned over time that she was right. Big John was soft spoken and quiet, and you never saw him lose his temper. To see him walk, you would never guess he was a runner. But when he ran, he had a smooth, beautiful stride that reminded me of a thoroughbred horse about to win the Kentucky Derby. He went on to become an absolute treasure to coach.

Mike McDonald came to White's from Gary, Ind., while in junior high, and he would remain there until he graduated. Mike had a tall, thin build and developed into a good athlete. At first, my biggest challenge with Mike was his attitude, although I had a lot of grace for these kids and all they had been through by the time I met them.

Our first official football practice was on Aug. 15, 1970. It was finally time to put on the pads and start working on our game. I tried hard not to laugh as I watched the players begin to dress for practice. Many of them had never put pads on before. After a bit of teasing from the holdover players, I stepped in and reminded the team that we'd all been in that situation before. I encouraged those teasing their teammates to step up and be leaders who are willing to help the players who needed assistance. But I must admit, it was a hilarious sight.

Dave Fulkerson, the head basketball coach and athletic director, would be my assistant coach for football. He was a tremendous support, helping me coach the offensive and defensive lines while I worked with our most skilled players. I was the offensive and defensive coordinator, and I had two volunteers who were teachers on campus. We were a small athletic staff, to say the least, but I was up for the challenge.

Our first football game was coming up in three weeks against Park Tudor, a private school in Indianapolis with a team full of well-to-do students. Our team looked forward to playing a team they considered to be "rich kids."

Most area schools held "two-a-day" practices while their students were out of school for the summer. Because White's held classes throughout the summer, our athletes had to practice twice each day in addition to attending classes. The schedule was tough. We held one practice immediately after their school day, which concluded at 3:10 p.m., then we walked to the cafeteria for a quick meal around 5:15. After eating, we went back to the practice field, where we would stretch again, hold a question-and-answer session, then get back to work. When the second practice was over, students went back to their divisions to study and go to bed.

One week before our first game, as I evaluated the kind of team we had, I went back to the advice a wise instructor had talked about in one of my college classes: KISS ... Keep It Simple, Stupid. It was clear that I needed to make things much simpler for these players. I changed our number system from "odd one side and even the other" to simply "right and left." I also cut down on the number of plays they needed to remember because they simply couldn't absorb them all.

There were a handful of eight or 10 players I felt good

about. I would depend on them to go both ways — offense and defense. I believed their speed would make up for inexperience. We couldn't afford any injuries. And, because White's was not a lockdown facility, there was often a problem with students running away, and we certainly couldn't afford any runaways without wreaking havoc on our team.

We had a kicker named Ken, who had a great leg. I started working on how to score extra points when we kicked. I asked them to line up and I faced the kicker, explaining to the linemen how to block. I instructed them to huddle up and go through the formation as if we were going through with the play, but not to kick the ball so I could see the linemen's footwork.

I looked directly at the kicker and said, "Everything live, but do not kick the ball."

"Okay," Ken responded.

They formed the huddle, came up to the line of scrimmage, barked the signal, and hiked the ball. I looked down at the linemen's feet, then *wham*. The football hit me square in the face and knocked me flat on the ground. Everything went silent and the players stared wide-eyed as I sat up, with blood pouring from my nose.

I was furious, but I had promised myself I would not curse in front of the players. I had a great coach in junior high school who taught me a lot of good things but always threw in a lot of offensive language, and I wanted to set a good example for these players. I held my tongue, but it wasn't easy.

Still wiping blood, I told them that would be the last time I would ever demonstrate how to block an extra point. When I dismissed them to get showered, the whole team quietly bolted for the locker room.

Once the players had cleared the field, I asked Coach Fulkerson to make sure the locker room was clear before I got in there. As I helped the managers pick up footballs and equipment from the field, one of them asked me if I was mad.

"What do you think?!" I asked.

Nothing else was said.

When the managers and I got back to the locker room, Coach

Fulkerson was the only one there. He told me none of the players had showered. Ken, the kicker, hadn't even changed out of his practice gear. He just grabbed his clothes and ran to his division.

Once the managers left, Coach Fulkerson and I were able to have a good laugh. I knew I needed to follow up with Ken, so I stopped by his division to check on him. I assured him that I wasn't going to hold this over his head but I needed him to listen better. Then, I jokingly told him if he couldn't kick hard enough to knock me completely out, he needed to work on his leg strength. We laughed and I hugged him, then went home for the night.

The next day, as the players were dressing for practice, an athlete named Ralph came into my office and asked if he could have a rooster.

"You need what?!" I asked.

"A rooster."

"Why on earth would you need a chicken?" I begged.

"No, Coach, I need a rooster that has our names, heights, and weights," he explained.

"You mean a roster?" I clarified, trying not to laugh.

"Yeah," he smiled.

I was beginning to realize how important a sense of humor would be. I was serious about the work, but I had to learn not to take myself too seriously for everyone's sake.

During the last week of preparations for our first game, I reflected a great deal on why I was there and what I could do to help those young men understand the value of teamwork. I reminded them of the opportunities White's could play in their futures. I acknowledged that most of them were not at White's because they chose to be, but encouraged them to give this experience a chance to improve their lives for years to come. I talked about the importance of teamwork, how to have each other's backs, and how their participation in this team could help them learn things they've never had a chance to experience before.

On the evening before our first game against Park Tudor,

our starting tailback got a finger in his eye during practice. He would not be able to play the next night.

As we ended that Thursday practice, one of the defensive backs came up and said, "Coach, we have a good secondary, but I'm not sure about our firstdary."

At first, I wondered if I heard him correctly, but I did. And he was not kidding. There was certainly never a dull moment with these guys. But he was right when he said we had a good secondary. I felt confident that our backup tailback would do well. The White's Warriors were as ready as we would ever be for the first game of our first season together.

CHAPTER FOUR
Year One of Coaching

The next night, we entered our home field for the first football game of the season. I would learn that, before every home game at White's, the national anthem was always sung by the school's English teacher, Ms. Hilda Clarke. Hilda was affectionately called "Miss Chicken" by the students because she called all the girls little chickens. Ms. Clarke would become a lifelong friend to me and my family; however, I never did learn why she called the students chickens.

During that first season opener, we went up against Park Tudor from Indianapolis with an excited team and a nervous coach. The boys played an outstanding game and won 42-0! We were a happy bunch.

The following Friday, we made the 90-mile trip to Indianapolis to face the Indiana School for the Deaf. Our scouting report stated that they were well-coached and played hard, and it was our first away game. I wondered how we would fare on the road.

During our previous game, I had called the plays by sending them in with my offensive right guards. But for this game, I called out the plays to the quarterback.

The first time we got the ball, I called out, "Thirty-eight, sweep left!" The whole opposing defense met our tailback and we lost yardage.

Next, I called, "Counter trap right!" And they stopped us again.

After calling the next pass play, I noticed their defensive end watching me, then hand-signaling to the rest of his teammates. And that was the moment I realized he was reading my lips and tipping off their defense!

I quickly went back to alternating my offensive guards and sending them in with the next play. Lesson learned.

The School for the Deaf was tough and gritty, but we beat them 28-0. I later became a big fan of this team but I know we were lucky to get out of Indianapolis with a 2-0 record.

Next up would be our rival team from Northfield High School, one of our county's public high schools. The Monday before that game, several excited players came to me saying, "Alley Cat is back! Alley Cat is back!"

I asked Coach Fulkerson to fill me in. He explained that Elix Brewer was returning to White's. He had attended back in junior high and was popular with the students and staff alike. Then he mentioned that Elix was a good athlete.

"Great! I like good athletes!" I responded.

Coach went on to tell me how Mr. Curless had been driving in Indianapolis and, as he was passing Victory Field, he saw Elix hitchhiking. He stopped and picked him up and, during the next few minutes, Elix expressed that he wanted to come back to White's because he was afraid he wouldn't graduate if he stayed in Indianapolis. He went on to explain how wanted the opportunity to go to college and become a successful person.

Mr. Curless reminded him students couldn't just come to White's at will. They had to be sent by the court system.

Elix's first experience at White's began in 1967, after he had spent a year at the Indianapolis Juvenile Center, often referred to as "The Hill." His probation officer sent him to White's and, at the time, he wasn't happy about it. But after three or four months, he was making friends and had discovered a new way of life where he didn't have to steal money for food or entertainment.

He had been placed in Division #4, which was a dormitory-style building. Each night, when it was time for lights out, students were expected to stay in their assigned beds and no talking or reading was allowed. Elix earned the trust of his houseparent and was soon given the duty of monitoring the emergency door, which was marked by a bright exit light near his bed. He was allowed to read for as long as he wanted using the light from the exit sign.

He later recalled looking up at that glowing exit sign and thinking what a sweet deal he was able to get at "The Tute." He was enjoying three meals a day, recreation at the gym, and the school was in the process of building a swimming pool, bowling alley, and canteen where students could get ice cream and other treats. He had everything he needed without having to steal for it.

After Mr. Curless's encounter with Elix in Indianapolis during that summer of 1970, Elix went to his probation office to ask if he could be sent to White's again. The officer explained how the court system has to make that decision. So, two nights later, Elix broke into an appliance store and held a portable television in his arms until the police department arrived to arrest him. That was the only way he knew for sure how to find his way back to the one place he knew would offer him a better life and promising future.

The day I met Elix, after his return to White's, I observed a slight young man who was not taller than five-foot-six inches and weighed about 140 pounds. He was the same size I was at his age. I told him he could workout with the team but I had to hold off letting him play until the Indiana High School Athletic Association (IHSAA) verified that he was eligible.

That week's Friday night game against our county rivals at Northfield went much like our first two games. White's Warriors beat the Norsemen 31-7. We were ecstatic to have a 3-0 record.

The following week, however, I found out why a winning season at White's was not an expectation. Several players were dismissed for disciplinary reasons and two of our key players ran away, leaving us with a skeleton team.

We had another big county rival the following Friday with

Southwood, another local public school. The guys fell to Southwood 46-30, but they gave it a good effort.

My dad generously offered money to take the team out to eat. We needed some time together just to have fun, away from football, so I was grateful to be able to treat the team to Swedish Smorgasbord, an all-you-can-eat buffet for one price. We might not have been the greatest football team, but boy we could eat! If competitive eating had been our sport, we would have definitely gone undefeated. In fact, the restaurant ended up closing early that night because they ran out of food.

We lost three more starting players the following week for disciplinary reasons, bringing our total lost starters to six. Then we lost another starter after he was kicked in the throat and stopped breathing. Thank goodness for the CPR training I received at Ball State.

We hosted Caston for our next game of the season. They had lost their previous five games, and we added another loss to their season with a 16-0 win after Bill Jones scored two touchdowns, bringing his total to nine touchdowns for the season. He ended up leading the county in scoring, and Greg Boaz came in second.

With our depleted roster, we lost our next game against a team from Payne, Ohio, 32-12, and closed out the season with a 27-0 loss to Carroll High School in Fort Wayne. We finished the first season with a record of four wins and four losses, having only four of the starters we had at the beginning of the season.

Since our three-win start at the beginning of our first season, we had faced tough odds with runaways and injuries. But, even with guys going missing and the challenges of disciplinary action that made coaching so challenging at White's, there was one realization I learned during that first year: I could coach! Regardless of our win-loss record, I considered that first season of football a success.

I remained optimistic and took every possible opportunity to put positive thoughts into the players' minds. I reminded them often how lucky they were to be at White's and hoped they would look at their stay as a positive, not a negative. If nothing else, I wanted them to understand the importance of a winning attitude, whether or not our team would become a winning team.

After football season came basketball season, where I would be the assistant coach for Coach Fulkerson. His varsity basketball team finished that season 17-6. The junior varsity, comprised of all freshmen, had an 8-10 season and won a four-team holiday tournament. Not a bad season, considering all the factors White's coaches and players face during a typical season.

Then, after basketball season, came time for my first season coaching track. The cinder track at White's was in bad shape. If we had any rain at all it became a nightmare. Tracks built before the 1980s were always 440 yards per lap in length. Later, they began using 400 meters as the measure of a lap and school tracks were built to that specification. We still used yards at that point, and our team would run the mile relay, which has since been replaced by the 1600-meter relay. The mile relay is about 9.3 meters longer than the 1600-meter relay.

I had 20 athletes who came out for track, only 10 of whom could score. It was during that season, with only three weeks remaining, I decided to abandon the beat-up old track at White's. Instead, we started practicing on the U-shaped driveway next to the school's administration building. It was not ideal, but it was an improvement over the weather-beaten remains of the track we had been using.

That season we ended up beating six schools and losing to four. Elix Brewer was the leader in points, and John Maggott was third. We scored a few points in the Huntington track sectional, but all things considered, the first season coaching track was disappointing.

Looking back at that season, as I self-evaluated, I knew I had done the right thing by moving off the old track. But, with or without a track, I believed I could build a strong track team in the years ahead.

After the first year at White's, I was determined to take what I had learned and keep looking ahead to find ways we could make the most of what, and who, we had.

CHAPTER FIVE
On the Right Track

Graduation and transfers wiped out the 1970 football squad after the first year, so I spent the summer focusing on weight training, conditioning, and trying to lay strong groundwork for the following year. If nothing else, I wanted to help the students develop character, become stronger, learn to work as a team, and gain confidence, regardless of our win-loss record.

I often shared with them the phrases I had often put into practice, both as an athlete and in my daily life:

"Rise to the occasion."

"When all is said and done, there is more said than done."

"You have to believe to achieve."

"If you speak to God, He will hear you, and if you don't hear God, you aren't listening."

"It's possible if you believe."

Every chance I got, I poured positive thoughts into the players' minds, hoping they were as meaningful for them as they had been to me.

Outside the athletic department office hung a poster of legendary UCLA coach John Wooden's Pyramid of Success, which focuses on the building blocks of good character, self-control, team spirit, and attitude, to eventually create successful outcomes. The principles apply not only to athletic success, but to any area of life. I had hung the poster shortly after arriving at White's.

The first year teaching and coaching at White's had reminded me of the importance of those building blocks, even in my own life. Keeping my enthusiasm up required me to stay connected to my colleagues and mentors as I took on the challenges of leading these young athletes.

White's was built around a family model and, though Christian values were modeled and encouraged for the students, faith was not pushed down their throats. I was grateful to work with good, dedicated people who wanted the best for the students.

I also got to know the local track and football coach at nearby Southwood High School, John Livergood, who became a great friend and source of support. I also stayed in contact with my former coaches and mentors.

When my second football season at White's began, I had 32 players who made it through pre-season. However, only five of those players had any experience playing football.

Elix brought speed at the tailback position. I placed John Maggott at fullback and Mike McDonald at split-end. This combination would place our strongest players in key positions and I felt we were as ready as we could be to begin our second season.

Our first game would be against Park Tudor and, just as we were boarding the bus for the two-hour trip to Indianapolis, I saw Mr. Curless bounding toward the bus. The look on his face told me he was not bringing good news.

He proceeded to call the names of five players (three starters and two backup players) to come with him. He told me they were in trouble back in their housing unit and would not be going to the game. Our season started with a loss to Park Tudor that night.

Midway through the season, we got a new student on the team named James Brashers. He was a big kid, so I asked Coach Fulkerson to take him for the [defensive] line. About 20 minutes into his first practice, I heard Coach's voice raise and looked over to see what was going on. He was telling Brashers to start running over to the track and not to stop.

Brashers jogged in that direction for a moment, then started walking. Coach then yelled, so Brashers could hear, that if he didn't start running, Coach was going to send the rest of the linemen to run after him.

Suddenly Brashers kicked into gear and started running as fast as he could go. Boy, he was fast! I couldn't help but smile. I yelled across the field for Coach Fulkerson to leave that running back alone and send him back to me.

James, whom we called Jim, turned out to be extremely coachable. He became the hardest worker in the weight room I ever coached and, before long, had a body shaped like a Greek god. I learned that Brashers' caseworker in Kalamazoo, Mich., had sent him to White's because he heard we had a good athletic program. I'd like to send a big thank you to that caseworker, wherever you are!

Regardless of the rough start, we went on to finish the 1971-72 football season with a respectable five wins, three losses, and one tie. Elix was the leading scorer in the county, with 15 touchdowns, and he rushed for 6.2 yards a carry. His best game was against Antwerp, Ohio, when he scored four touchdowns and gained 207 yards rushing in just 12 attempts.

At the start of our 1972 track season, Elix Brewer, John Maggott, Mike McDonald, were juniors in high school, and Jim Brashers was a sophomore. I planned on splitting them up during the regular season so two of them could run the 880-yard relay (220 yards each) and the other two would run the mile relay. We had some other good runners, so I was confident we could win both relays and improve team scores by splitting them between the two events. I would then put all four of them together for sectional and let them run the 880 relay, which they preferred. My plan, if all four were still at White's for the 1973 season, was to run them in the mile relay if I could make Brashers into a quarter-mile runner by the following year.

With that plan in mind, I set my sights on White's Institute winning the state championship in the mile relay. I knew my ambitions were high, but not impossible, and I trained the team accordingly.

Our track was a major problem. I'd been told White's once had a good cinder track; however, over the years it had eroded beyond repair. There was a county road that ran through the middle of the campus and our U-shaped drive came directly off the road. The makeshift track we used for practice included the driveway, which ran between the administrative office and Division 5, and a portion of the county road. This oval was 296 yards around. Dodging traffic on the county road was far from ideal, and the surface was old, but it was better than the battered track. We made it work.

For conditioning, they ran what I called "progressions and regressions." Progressions involved sprinting for 60 yards, then walking the same distance, then doubling the yardage, again alternating between sprinting and walking. With each progression, the yardage was doubled, and the exercise became increasingly more challenging as the yardage increased. Once they had sprinted and walked for 592 yards, regressions began, and the yardage decreased by half, ending with a final sprint and walk for 60 yards. After that drill, they ran to the hill for downhill running.

I believed downhill running drills would be beneficial for all the runners because it would help smooth out their gaits, but it would be especially beneficial for Brashers. He was a pure sprinter and a speed runner but he had trouble running more than 300 yards. The hill on the north edge of the school property was perfect for downhill running, so one of their drills became running downhill and walking back up several times in a row during practices. Most track drills involve running up a hill and walking down, but we were looking for smoothness and I had come to believe this approach could help them learn to run with less effort.

The school only owned four hurdles and I was concerned that we didn't have enough to give the team adequate training. But we worked with what we had and I trained them on form and steps the best I could. We were able to develop strong hurdlers. The only event that we weren't able to work on adequately was the pole vault due to a lack of equipment.

One of the team's favorite conditioning drills was tire racing, so I often saved that for the end. They tied one end of a rope around their waists and the other end to a heavy truck tire. The runners would then race one another around our oval makeshift track pulling the tires behind them. The track team loved contests and before long I nicknamed them "Road Warriors."

As a coach at White's, you never knew for sure who would be eligible to compete from one day to the next. Athletes could run off, get sent home, or get into trouble with their houseparents or school staff without warning. But I sincerely believed I would have my four runners for the entire 1972 season, and 1973 too. My biggest concern was keeping them out of trouble, especially Mike McDonald.

About half-way through the 1972 season, a houseparent called me, furious, because a couple of the players had not returned to their division after their post-practice showers. The students were always expected to walk together, as a group, directly to their divisions from the gym, where the showers were located. Elix didn't attend practice that day because he was not feeling well so, without him there to watch over them, some of the players strayed down to the girls divisions.

The next day before practice I parked the team bus beside the gym door and informed the players that, since I couldn't trust them to go back to their divisions like they were supposed to, I was going to drive them back myself. It probably seemed ridiculous to them, since the gym was only one block from their divisions, but I needed to make a point.

After a week of taking them by bus from the gym to their divisions, Elix told me he would make sure everyone went as a group. I trusted that he would. I was happy not to drive them back and the team was more than happy not to be driven. We never had a problem with players not going straight to their divisions after that week.

During my first season at White's, we had only competed against 10 schools and I knew we needed more competition. I asked Coach Fulkerson to schedule more meets and to try putting us up against bigger schools. He succeeded in scheduling us at twenty-four schools during the 1972 season, including some larger events that included several schools.

Our team that year consisted of 15 runners and, though we didn't have a lot of depth, I knew we had 15 guys with potential. We had a tough time in dual events, but we would be hard to beat in relays involving three or more teams.

One of the meets on our schedule took place at Madison-Grant High School, a new school that had been formed by consolidating my old high school in Fairmount with Summitville High School, which was just a few miles from Fairmount. The week of that meet, I warned the team we were going back to my hometown for a dual meet and I knew it would be tough for us to beat them. I urged the guys to do their best and make me proud. As it turned out, two of my best runners couldn't compete for disciplinary reasons, so I knew everyone else would have to run at their highest ability to have a chance.

The day of the meet against Madison-Grant arrived and it was cold, windy, and rainy outside. I'd had a rule from Day One at White's that, no matter what the weather, everyone had to take off their sweats before competing in a meet.

We ran a close meet and I was cautiously optimistic that we were about to win. I stood at the finish line as the runners started the 220-yard dash on the backstretch, and I fully expected Brashers and Elix to finish first and second, respectively But, just as the starting gun went off, I looked at my runners in shock. They were both running in rain-soaked sweats. They took second and third place in a race they should have easily finished in first and second place.

We lost the meet by two points.

"What were you guys thinking?!" I begged them after the race.

They apologized profusely and admitted they didn't think they could be defeated.

Coach Fulkerson had driven to Fairmount to watch the team compete and, as I was walking back to the bus formulating all the things I wanted to tell them on the drive back, he told me I had to go back to campus with him. He could see that I was upset and, by the time we reached the campus, I knew he had spared me from saying things I would regret. I loved those guys and I still do to this day. I knew what happened that day was a lesson they would not forget, nor would I.

When I walked into the gym after the drive back, Elix and Brashers were both waiting for me. With tears in their eyes, they hugged me. Nothing more was ever said about it, and nothing needed to be said.

As the date for the track sectional approached, I had a difficult decision to make. Mike McDonald was having problems in his housing unit and his teachers were telling me he wasn't doing well in school. I had this dream that we could have one of the top mile relay teams in the state of Indiana the following year, but he was a key part of making that dream a reality. He was a gifted runner. I was confident that he, along with Elix, Brashers, and Maggott, would still be at White's the following year. I made the decision to use an alternate runner, Tony Hamilton, in the 880-yard relay at sectional instead of Mike.

I talked with Mike and told him he needed to change both his attitude and his school performance if he wanted to be part of something special in the future. I got the other three guys together and let them know Mike would not be running in sectional and we all believed Tony was a strong runner who would do a good job.

We finished second place in the 880 relay in the sectional and qualified for regional in Fort Wayne, which would take place the following week. I spoke with Mike several times and he assured me he was getting his act together because he wanted to be a part of all the athletic teams the next year.

At the Fort Wayne regional, we beat the team that won first in the Huntington sectional. But then we were disqualified for passing the baton outside the passing zone. When we got back to White's that evening, I told Elix, Brashers, and Maggott that I wanted them to meet me in my office on Monday after school.

I asked Mike McDonald to be there, too.

When the guys got to my office that Monday afternoon, I finally told them my dream of winning state in the mile relay the following year. This was the first time I had ever verbalized to them how far I believed they could go.

Brashers immediately replied, "I can't run that far! I can't even run the 440!"

I turned to Elix and asked who else we could get to run instead of Brashers. Instantly Brashers changed his tune and decided he would try. I told him we could get him there physically, but he had to do the mental work and start believing he could do it.

Next, I broached a more difficult part of the conversation when I let them know the order in which they would be running. "Big John" Maggot had been the anchorman in every relay he had ever run, and he always had difficulty taking hand-offs. So, when I announced that he would be leading off, followed by Brashers, then McDonald, and then Elix, Big John was visibly upset.

"I'm always the anchorman," he argued.

"John, you're our best 440 man and we need you to get us the lead and put fear into the other team." I told him, knowing I had my work cut out for me during the next few weeks if I was going to convince him. This new order would mean a lot of extra work for Brashers, too.

I then reminded them that nobody else believed we could do this, but I knew we could if each of them did his part. Big John kept his head down but he was a team player and eventually came around. Especially after hearing a story that had happened a few years earlier in our state.

I asked the guys if they had ever heard of Milan High School. Elix said he had heard of it but didn't know much about their team. I explained how, in 1954, Milan was one of the smallest basketball teams in Indiana, yet they had beat one of the biggest schools to win the state championship. The 1986 movie, *Hoosiers*, was inspired by that upset. No one could have predicted that Milan High School would beat Muncie Central to win the 1954 Indiana High School State Championship.

Our track team winning the mile relay would be an even bigger accomplishment; however, we would have to beat nine of the biggest schools in our state at the same time! I wanted them to start thinking big about winning track, even in a basketball state like ours.

They already knew the importance of strength training and were dedicated to weight lifting. I often had to kick them out of the weight room. We spent the summer working on both weightlifting and conditioning. I also had a chance to get to know the guys better during those months.

Brashers had a home visit in Kalamazoo, Mich., that summer. Instead of sending him home on a bus, I decided to drive him up myself. My sister, Sue, and her family lived on a lake in Portage, which was just outside Kalamazoo. I arranged a stop there on our way up so we could spend a few hours boating, fishing, and eating with family. Brashers had a great time, and my niece and nephews thought he was the greatest. We then went the rest of the way to Kalamazoo where he could see his family. I enjoyed meeting them and I could tell they were happy to see him doing well.

I often brought Elix to Fairmount with me to visit my parents in Fairmount. Since both Becky's parents and mine still lived in Fairmount, we tried to go visit with them on Sunday evenings. We were grateful for our parents' much-needed moral support. My dad was a gifted musician, so the house was often filled with music, and my mother was a great cook. Each year we planted an acre of garden and we shared produce with anyone who needed anything. Naturally, as they got to know Elix, they considered them an extension of our family. My mother often sent him back to White's with a German Chocolate cake she had baked for him.

Reverend Darnell, the chaplain at White's, spent a lot of time with Elix. Reverend Darnell could see what a remarkable young man Elix was and mentored him spiritually. Elix not only chose to put his faith in God while attending White's, he also lived out his growing faith. I was glad to see a student with his influence making decisions that would give him a better future while also providing an example to other young men who looked up to him.

I felt like we were on the right track. I hoped sharing my dream and my time with the runners would help them see what I could see in them. They had all experienced past circumstances that could have negatively affected them for the rest of their lives; but I wanted them to see beyond their past and into a bright, hopeful future. That was often easier said than done, but I remained hopeful.

CHAPTER SIX
Another Tough Season

I was looking forward to the fall of the 1972-1973 year, because I knew we had a lot of football players coming back. However, a staggering number of students went AWOL (short for "absent without leave"). Among the students who ran away were several of my key football players.

Most of the students were found and returned to campus within a few days, but it was hard on my ego after all the time I'd spent working with them. I hoped I wasn't wasting my energy trying to create a team they could be proud of and helping them understand the opportunities White's could offer them. I prayed every night for guidance to teach the athletes that winning in life is more important than any athletic victory.

Whenever we had students go AWOL, Coach Fulkerson would come to our house to get me, and we would round up some of our athletes to help us find the runaways. Coach Fulkerson had once been a student at White's. He knew how the "runners" thought. He also knew the local spots where "runners" were most likely to show up. He would drop off our athletes in those places, then he and I would go to the local donut shop, drink coffee, eat sweets, and wait. Ninety percent of the time, by the time we got back to the locations where the athletes had been dropped off, the "runners" would be there waiting for us, too. Coach Fulkerson rarely guessed incorrectly.

As the start of football season approached, we got most of our runners back but we were still missing players in key positions. Anytime a player ran away, he would have to miss two games. For that reason, the season that could have been a winning season for us turned out to be one of the most challenging.

We would face Union City High School in our first game of the season. This team had some of the best running backs in the state, including Rick Ennis, who would become an outstanding running back at Indiana University a few years later. I knew we would have a difficult time winning against Union City with our depleted team.

The week before that game, we faced another setback. Elix suffered a shoulder injury during practice that would keep him from starting the season as our running back. I moved Brashers to tailback from his usual fullback position and moved Big John from tight end to fullback. Elix spent the days leading up to our game against Union City helping Brashers learn the tailback plays. Although we didn't have his physical help, we leaned on his leadership ability to help us get ready.

Then we received more bad news. Coach Fulkerson was sent to Colorado to retrieve some of our runaways, so we would not have our assistant coach. Fortunately, I had a volunteer coach, Darrell Boone, who had been working with Fulkerson as an assistant line coach. He and his wife were houseparents at White's and cared deeply for the students. He would join me in the matchup against Union City and we would do the best we could given the circumstances.

We got behind early and lost to Union City 28-8, but Mike McDonald caught a 14-yard touchdown pass from our quarterback, Mike Castle. Big John caught a conversion pass to account for our eight points, and Brashers gained 86 yards rushing. We held Ennis to 76 yards rushing, 47 of which came on a fourth-quarter run. We only gave up six points during the second half, and our tackle, Dave Joseph, and linebacker, Scott Yano, gave great defensive efforts. So, all things considered, I was proud of how we played.

After that loss, Principal Lew Curless made the team a promise. If they won the rest of the games that season, he would let them shave his head. I believed they had it in them, but with the challenges we faced on a weekly basis, we would have to work harder than ever and we couldn't keep losing players.

Our next game would be against the Indiana School for the Deaf. We learned that some of our players would have to sit out the game because they had violated school policies, and Elix was still out with his shoulder for at least another game. I had no problem getting the remaining team members to take this match-up seriously, especially after our previous experiences with this team. This game would require our best efforts. The guys had to fight hard but, in the end, eked out an 18-8 victory after three very close quarters against the hard-hitting team from Indianapolis.

We then had two weeks to prepare for our next opponent, LaPorte LaLumiere, which was a small private school with a consistently strong football team. Their linebacker, John Roberts, was an excellent player who would later become the Chief Justice of the United States Supreme Court.

Winning against the LaLumiere Leopards would break our six-year losing streak against them, so I was glad to learn that Elix would be back and our team would be at full strength. I couldn't wait to see how our backfield performed when we had both Brashers and Elix, along with Big John, McDonald, and Manual Jewell as wide receivers. We had big, fast linemen and linebackers.

We scored first after McDonald caught a 30-yard pass from our quarterback, Mike Castle. Next, Elix took a punt and ran 90 yards for a touchdown. Dang, it was good to have him back. Then Brashers went 75 yards from the line of scrimmage to take us to an 18-0 lead at half-time.

During the second half, Tony Hamilton went 72 yards from the scrimmage line for a touchdown. Then Big John closed out the scoring with a 45-yard pass from backup quarterback, Terry Bunch. We won against the Leopards 32-0 and our defense never let LaLumiere get closer than our 16-yard line. The 105-mile trip back to Whites was a happy one for both the

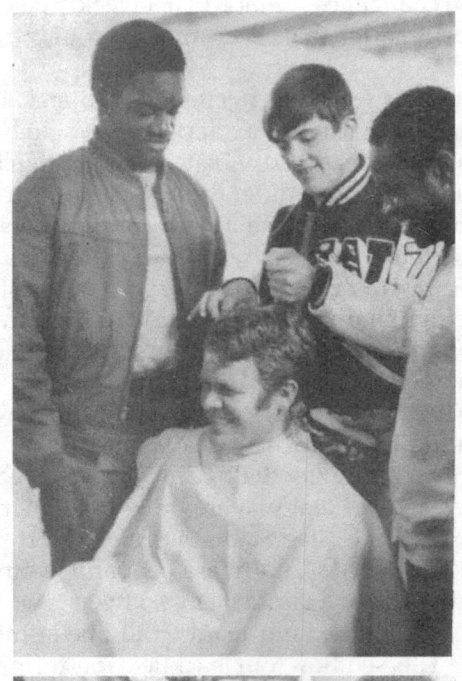
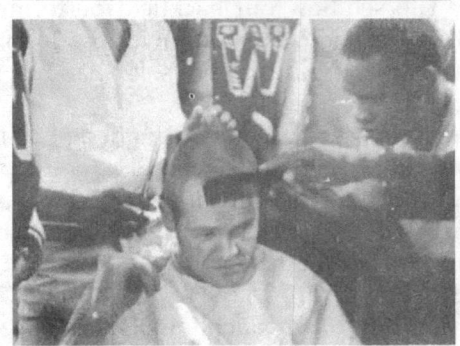

Keeping his promise for a season of victories is Principal Lewis Curless

team and coaches.

Our next game was against our county rivals, Southwood High School, who had humiliated us the year before with a 50-0 win. After that game, I had made a promise to a local sports reporter that they would regret leaving their starters in during the fourth quarter. I intended to fulfill my promise that week.

Four days of heavy rain the week before that game turned our football field into a mess. Southwood's athletic director called to tell me their coach wanted to move the game to their field. I politely declined.

That week, while we practiced on a terrible field with its south end covered in water, I put last year's score up on the scoreboard. After warmups, I asked the team to turn toward the scoreboard and chant, "Hate that score!"

When game time came, I was glad we had Brashers. He had a stable base and was one of the only players on the field who could run well in bad conditions.

We took a 12-0 lead in the first half. Before beginning the second half of the game, the refs and Southwood's coach asked if we could play only on the north end of the field. I asked their coach which half they were starting on during the second half, but I already knew the answer. He told me they were supposed to start on the south end.

"Well, you better get your team down there because that is the end of the field we're kicking off to," I informed him.

We held Southwood under a hundred yards of total offense during both halves. Brashers ran for 167 yards in 13 carries. Elix ran for 31 yards in five carries. McDonald and Brashers both had interceptions, and Brashers ran his in for 61 yards and scored a touchdown. We won 18-6.

After Southwood's team boarded their bus and headed home, my White's Warriors lined up on our messy field and pointed to the scoreboard, chanting together, "Love that score!"

We continued our winning streak the following week against Caston High School. We won 12-0 on our field, which was still in poor condition.

Next, we would face rival Northfield on their field. I got word that Northfield's coach had made a negative comment to his team about the White's Warriors. Coach Jim Kaltenmark was a class guy and one of my very favorite coaches. But I knew how to light a fire under my team. I may have embellished his comment a bit when I shared with the team that our opponent's coach didn't think our team was very good.

On the first play of the game, Northfield threw us for a one-yard loss. I then called a reverse to Elix and, 31 seconds into the game, he went for a 74-yard touchdown. When Northfield got the ball, they fumbled on the 40-yard line. Six plays later and we were in the end zone when Tony Hamilton scored on a 13-yard sweep.

With four minutes and 30 seconds remaining in the first quarter, Brashers took a pitchout and swept right end for an 81-yard score. On a White's punt, with four minutes and 47 seconds left in the first half, Northfield fumbled and White's Larry Thein recovered in the endzone to bring the score to 27-0 at halftime. We already had 297 yards rushing by halftime.

The third quarter was scoreless. Northfield's defense played much better during the second half But, during the fourth quarter, with nine minutes and 39 seconds left on the clock, Northfield scored and brought the score to 27-6. They tried an onside kick and we recovered on Northfield's 48-yard line. We lost six yards on the first two plays, then I put our backup quarterback, Terry Bunch, in the tailback position. A halfback option pass of 55 yards went to a speeding Mike McDonald, who scored and brought the score to 34-6.

We had two punts blocked late in the game, which Northfield turned into scoring opportunities. With a total of 95 yards of penalties in the second half, we still pulled out a 34-20 victory. On the bus ride back to White's after the game, I told the team I was disappointed with our second half, but also reminded them that we had beat a strong team with one of the best coaches in the area.

Next up was Antwerp High School from Ohio at White's. Brashers scored five touchdowns and we took a 48-0 score into halftime. We played reserves during the second half and defeated Antwerp 54-14 with a total of 351 yards rushed.

We traveled to North Miami High School, about 35 miles west of Whites, for the last game of the season. During the first quarter, Brashers scored three touchdowns and Big John scored on a fumble recovery which brought us to a 26-0 lead by the end of the quarter.

During the second period, Elix ran for a 45-yard score and Brashers added the two-point conversion. North Miami scored its lone touchdown of the game on a 60-yard pass play during that quarter, and Brashers then took the kickoff back 85 yards for a 42-7 score at halftime.

By the end of that game, Brashers scored five touchdowns for the second straight week and ran for 172 yards rushing in 12 carries. Tony Hamilton gained 98 yards in eight carries, and Elix ran 51 yards in five carries. We recovered three fumbles and intercepted a total of six passes. Each intercepted by a different player. Andre Cothen, McDonald, Brashers, Nate Truvillion, Ralph Thomas, and Manuel Jewell each had an interception. The final score was 68-9.

After we returned from North Miami, Principal Curless met the team at the Canteen and they enthusiastically gathered around him to shave his head. A story ran in the local paper, along with photos of the celebratory shave, and we were pleased to finish our best season yet.

Even through bad days and tough seasons, I was moved by the dedication of so many of the White's staff members. Students didn't just get an education and a chance to participate in sports, the staff cared for them as individuals.

"Miss Chicken" was one of those exceptional people. During her English classes, students learned more than the basics of grammar. She taught them how to make a difference in the world. During the Gulf War, she and her English class wrote so many letters to soldiers that General Norman Schwarzkopf sent her a handwritten thank-you letter. She wasn't born in America; she was born and raised in Honduras and Spanish was her native language. But the school couldn't have found a better English teacher anywhere.

I was also grateful for the ongoing support of my friend, Jim Law, who made good on the promise he'd made to support me if I accepted the job at White's. Each year he asked me for a list of students who needed extra love and support at Christmas. Then, he and a group of students from Fellowship of Christian Athletes came to White's bearing gifts for the students. They didn't just drop off the gifts. They spent hours bowling, swimming, and getting to know the students who weren't able to go home to a supportive family over the Christmas holidays. Despite of the challenges, there were so many reasons to be hopeful about the good things happening in students' lives as a result of this special place. I fully believed these kids could do anything they wanted with their lives and I wanted more than anything for *them* to believe it.

CHAPTER SEVEN
Track Season 1973

Most of the guys went straight from football season into basketball season. The varsity basketball team finished that 1972-1973 season with a 12-10 record and the junior varsity record was 15-5. Brashers had been voted the MVP and led Wabash County in scoring with 492 points. Elix was the top free-throw shooter and led the team in assists.

Since they had been playing hard through two seasons, I decided to start track practice two weeks later than usual. I felt the students needed some downtime. Even if it affected our chances in the Wabash County meet, I hoped the time would ultimately make the team stronger for the Huntington sectional.

Coach Fulkerson was really good at motivating his team. I told him I didn't want our relay team to be overly cocky, but I wanted them to walk into meets with confidence this year. A few days later, Coach came up with a classic Fulkerson idea. He brought in black leather jackets with large white lettering on the back that said, "Speed Specialties, Inc." At first, they looked like jackets a motorcycle gang would wear, so we decided to put "White's High" under the lettering and added the guys' names to the front of their jackets. Needless to say, they absolutely loved them.

At the start of the 1973 track season, I had finally convinced Big John that he was the best runner to lead off the relay, and Mike McDonald had become a better student. But I still needed to get Brashers to believe that he could become an outstanding 440-yard runner.

During one of our Sunday evenings at my parents' house, Dad and I were sitting in the backyard swing talking about the upcoming track season. I expressed to him that I needed to get Brashers to believe in his ability to be a strong 440 runner. Dad sat there a minute, then went into the house. After a short time, he came back out carrying a large jar of honey.

"Give this to Brashers and tell him to eat a teaspoon of this honey before he runs," Dad said as he handed the jar to me.

"Do you really think this will make him a good 440 runner?" I asked Dad.

"If *he* believes it does, that's what matters," Dad replied.

Early in the season, we had a meet at Tri-Central and this would be the first time Brashers ate honey before the meet. I told him it would give him more energy and he would be able to run anything.

Brashers ran a 9.8-second 100-yard dash that day, then he ran a 51.3 split in the mile relay. When we got back to White's and everyone finished showering, I met with the team and then asked if there were any questions.

Elix had a question: "Can the rest of us eat honey, too?"

So, after that, eating honey before each meet became part of our team's pre-game ritual.

One of our favorite drills was the goose step, which is often used during army training. The runners got a kick out of me when I showed them how it went, and we often ended practice with goose steps, which everyone enjoyed. It was these moments, when we just enjoyed the process of preparing for the season, that reminded me that those seasons at White's were about something bigger than learning to be competitive in track.

However, I knew if we could stay clear of injuries, runaways, and bad attitudes, we had the potential for an outstanding track season. McDonald had become a great hurdler and, even though we did not have a lot of equipment, we made the most of the school's four hurdles to work on good form. Brashers and Elix were our strongest sprinters, Big John was a strong starter in the longer 440-yard dash; Manuel Jewell mastered long jump, high jump, and hurdles; Rick Mills did shot-put and discus. Mike Dudley ran the 880 and relays.

That season we competed against 21 teams, most of which were from schools with 400 to 600 students. Though we had 18 wins and only three losses, I wanted the four relay runners to have a bigger event to help prepare them for the mile relay in sectional. We got that opportunity when we were invited to run in the Logansport Relays.

At Logansport, we gained a large lead early, then Elix ran at three-quarter speed until he got to the backstretch. Then, just as a runner from Kokomo High School began to close in, Elix started doing the goose step, then the stutter step, before sprinting to the finish line! That was a total surprise to me, but boy did I love seeing that. We beat Kokomo by six seconds and I knew my belief in my mile relay team was well-founded. We were as ready as we would ever be for sectional.

I drove the bus to Huntington North High School, while Brashers sat in the stairwell eating his honey. Then the rest of the guys took their turn getting honey. We were ready. As the guys exited the bus, I told them one last time that if each athlete did his part, we could win this meet.

Out of 20 teams competing in 15 events at sectional, we steamrolled our way to the top in five of those events, scoring a total of 81 points, which placed us in first place. Huntington (a school of 1,500 students) and Manchester tied for second place with 49 points each.

We easily won the mile relay, setting a new meet record of 3:23:0. Manuel Jewell won the long jump. Brashers won the 100-yard dash, and Elix came in third. Big John won the 440 in his personal best time. Mike McDonald won the low hurdles and broke the White's Institute record. Rick Mills placed third in the discus and broke a White's record. Mike Castle surprised everyone by placing sixth place in the discus throw and breaking an old White's record, as well.

While I knew we could win sectionals I had no idea we

would win with that kind of margin. I took a proud and happy team back to White's to celebrate.

Next, it was time to talk about the regional at Northrup in Fort Wayne. Feeding into the Fort Wayne regional would be qualifiers from the Fort Wayne, Huntington, Elkhart, and Kokomo sectionals.

During the week leading up to regionals, we spent a lot of time on relay hand-offs. I kept the tone fun and focused on the goal of doing our best to win the day.

Elix and Big John both qualified for state in individual events, and all the guys did well. Mills set a new county record in the discus but wasn't able to qualify for the finals.

The race of the night was the mile relay. Fort Wayne Northrop was favored to win, and their anchorman was Rick Magley, the best mile runner in the state. Big John gave us a lead with a 49.8-second run. Brashers then took our sizable lead further with an identical 49.8 leg. McDonald then took the third leg and kept our lead going with a 49.9 leg. Elix took over on the anchor leg and ran his relaxed three-quarter speed gait to the backstretch. Then, just as Magley began to close in and the Northrop crowd was going wild, Elix once again went into his now-famous stutter step before sprinting to the finish line for an easy White's win, bringing our relay time to 3:19. That time would convert to a 3:17.8 finish in today's 1600-meter relay.

Most people thought Gary West was the best mile relay team in the state after they won Its regional with a 3:20.1 and won its sectional with a 3:17:4 time. But our final time at our state regional placed us in Lane No. 1 at the state meet.

I had been checking the long-range weather for the state meet ever since the regionals, and everything pointed to a blazing hot, humid day. I told the team we would be practicing in the heat of the day at nearby Southwood High School to help prepare them to run in the heat.

One day while we were working out at Southwood, their football coach, Felix Chambers, came over to say that we were doing a great job, but we were about to run against men in Indianapolis.

"They grow studs at Gary West," he told me.

"We've got a Gary boy on our team, Mike McDonald, and I wouldn't trade him," I remarked.

He walked away chuckling.

I called the team over and told them Coach Chambers didn't think we could match up against Gary West and the other big teams in Indy.

Elix then pointed out that Coach Chambers didn't think we could beat Southwood in football either, but we had proved him wrong. We all laughed and went back to work.

I worked them hard early in the week. One morning I asked them to take a run on their own and reflect on what a wonderful thing was happening to them ... to remember how blessed they were. On Thursday, they got up at 5 in the morning and ran eight miles. They realized they were on a mission and their dedication was evident. Then, on Friday, we did a light workout and practiced hand-offs. At the end of that week, we felt ready and looked forward to Indianapolis.

When the big day arrived, we pulled into the parking lot at North Central High School in Indianapolis ready to face our competition, and, of course, we were armed with honey. I ran into my old track coach, Coach McAnally, from Fairmount, who was coaching for a large school in Michigan City, Ind. He was a good coach and an even better person, who had taught me a lot.

Coach McAnally said, "I see you have a fine relay team here!" But then he added, "I don't want to discourage you, but Gary West has an amazing team that I'm not sure anybody in the country could beat."

I told him that we came to win. Then he patted me on the shoulder and said, "That's what I expected you to say."

I was confident that, if the race was close when Elix got the baton for the final lap, nobody in the state could beat him. In a meet earlier in the season we were behind and he ran a 47.9 split for the win. I knew he had wheels.

Coaches were not allowed to go onto the field with the athletes during the state tournament. We sat in the bleachers where the rest of the spectators sat. So, before the team parted from me to walk onto the field, I reminded them to stay in the shade and only eat the food we brought for the team. I took Elix aside and charged him with keeping an eye out for the rest of the team.

About halfway through the meet, I noticed Elix standing at the fence motioning for me to come down. I could only assume something was wrong. I made my way to the fence where Elix stood on the other side and he told me Brashers and McDonald were eating hot dogs with the other athletes.

I sent Elix to tell them to get their butts over to the fence immediately. A few minutes later, here they came. Although it was too late to catch them before they ate junk food, I gave them a piece of my mind and sent them back to the field. Their relay was coming up and I hoped they were up for it.

Big John led off and brought us to a 10-yard lead before a good hand-off to Brashers, who maintained the lead coming around the final curve. But then I saw him start to struggle and before long he was blowing chunks of hotdog. But he hung in there and handed off to McDonald. Mike ran the race of his life and gave Elix a sizable lead.

When Elix got to the backstretch, none other than Rick Magley was coming for him. Magley had already won the mile run earlier and it seemed everyone in attendance expected him to pull ahead and win. Just then, a familiar scene played out.

Elix began his stutter-step before pulling away and speeding across the finish line for a Warriors' win! Our hard work in the bad heat paid off and, with the exception of a certain hot dog incident, we fared better than most of the runners in the high heat that day. Our time of 3:22:2 was outstanding considering the heat. Northrop was runner-up and Gary West failed to place.

After the team was awarded medals for their first-place finish in the mile relay, Coach Fulkerson had another surprise. Hiding under blankets in the van, he broke out trophies he'd ordered for the guys with "First Place State Champs Mile Relay" engraved on them.

As we traveled back to White's from Indianapolis, so many thoughts raced through my mind. Those young men were finally seeing in themselves something they hadn't seen before. I had seen it, and I wasn't sure if they had bought into what I'd been trying to tell them until that day. They weren't full of themselves, but they had accomplished something together that they might once have thought was impossible.

Early during my first year at White's, Coach Fulkerson had asked me what I thought it took to have a great team. I answered, "Ninety-percent great athletes and ten percent good coaching." But a lot could happen within that 10 percent. I had great athletes but I had to be careful not to mess them up. Just as I believed in them, I know they believed in me, too. They knew I would never ask them to do anything I wouldn't do myself. And the more I coached those young men, the more I enjoyed being around them.

Three weeks after the state finals, Mr. Robert Curless took me to breakfast in town and talked to me about my future. He said he knew there were bigger schools interested in me coaching for them. He told me to decide if I wanted to make a name for myself as a coach or if I wanted to help young people who needed someone like me in their lives. To me, that choice was easy. He knew I loved White's as much as he did. Needless to say, I stayed at White's.

After that 1973 season, I became the athletic director at White's Institute and spent the next 27 years in that capacity. Every year, when we played our basketball sectional at Huntington North, I would always look up at their track sectional banners hanging around the gym. This school of 1,500 students had won sectionals every year but one. The banner for 1973 was missing because it was displayed at "the Tute."

CHAPTER EIGHT
Where Are They Now?

When I told Elix I would be writing this book, he reflected on May 27th and June 6th of 1973 as two of the most special days of his life. Those were the dates of his graduation and state championship and they are forever sealed in his memory. He wrote down a few thoughts, including the following:

As our team captain for the "Speed Specialty Incorporated" foursome, I found it very hard containing their excitement about graduating and keeping my teammates motivated and focused on the upcoming meet. However, I thank God that we had Chuck Gaither as our track coach, who came up with unorthodox ways to train three "knuckleheads" who didn't want to train because it was too hot outside. And some of us thought, since we were undefeated and ran the fastest time in the regionals, we shouldn't have to practice that hard! But I must give a "shout out" to the house parents and staff members at White's who let the four of us walk around campus and go into town with little or no supervision.

After winning the state mile relay, it hit me that high school was over and I was on my own. However, Mike McDonald, John Maggott, and I were able to live with a family in Wabash, during the summer months before starting college, which eased our burden and helped us prepare for college. Mike McDonald went to IUPUI in Fort Wayne, John Maggott accepted a track scholarship to Middle Tennessee State, I went to Marion College (Indiana Wesleyan University); Brashers had one more year left of high school.

During 1973-1976 I ran track and played soccer and basketball for Marion College (IWU)... In 1978, God really blessed me. I was married in May to my beautiful wife, Elva Brewer.

Elix has now been married to Elva for over 40 years. He is retired and his family resides in McKinney, Texas, and he has often joined me on the golf course during the past few years. His goal is to beat me one of these days. I keep telling him to hang onto that dream, but it may not happen until I'm in my 90s. I am grateful we have been able to keep in touch.

After graduation from White's High School, James Brashers moved to a junior college in Iowa. The coaches at Middle Tennessee State had helped him get there, but after he had been there a few weeks I got a call from him. He said he didn't think the coaches at his new school liked him and he wasn't happy. I advised him to hang in there and I would see if I could get some time off to come and see him. The next night, before I could make arrangements, he showed up at our front door. He later joined the United States Army and attended Indiana State University. He now lives in Kalamazoo, Mich.

Although Mike McDonald and I fell out of touch over the years, I will always feel a connection with him because he was part of something very special. I was proud of the way he rose to the occasion and got his attitude in check by the time he was a senior. For that reason, he became a key to our relay success. His third leg in the State Final relay was crucial to our victory. I continue to hold out hope that Mike and I will have an opportunity to reconnect in the future.

I'm now retired and spend a good part of my time on the golf course. My experiences coaching at White's and watching those four young men become state champions are among the most treasured memories of my life.

I will forever carry those young men in my heart and I marvel at what we did together that year. Taking 12 athletes to the Huntington North sectional and beating 19 other teams, then going on to win the mile relay at the State Finals was, to me, a miracle for so many reasons. And, like every miracle, I can't take the credit. I know all our lives were changed. Our school still treasures that moment in its history.

I am incredibly proud of those four athletes and many other students who went on to make wonderful contributions to society after attending White's. They have become good parents, business owners, educators, soldiers, and citizens.

And remember the young woman who stopped me on my first day of work and shocked me into questioning whether or not I was cut out for the work ahead? Becky befriended that young woman and invited her to our home many times for meals, to watch television, and to let her enjoy the atmosphere of a safe, loving family. Our girls enjoyed getting to know her and considered her a family friend.

As for "Miss Chicken" (Hilda Clarke), when the time came for her to retire, White's school, board members voted unanimously to allow her to live on campus indefinitely. She doesn't have family nearby, so she has become an adopted member of our family. Becky and I have made plans for her to be buried next to us someday. In 2020, she turned 83 years old and still lived on campus happily. And, in my opinion, no singer's rendition of the National Anthem will ever top hers. We still visit her often and are grateful for the many ways she has impacted our lives and many others.

White's Institute is now known as White's Residential and Family Services. Though they have dropped their athletic program from the Indiana High School Athletic Association, the school still offers an exceptional experience where young people have the opportunity to learn and grow beyond what they previously thought possible.

Throughout the decades that have passed since Josiah White's estate first funded the purchase of that stretch of Indiana farmland, I believe the school's original founder would be pleased with how his vision has been carried out. Hundreds of students have received a new start, met people who believed in them, and were given access to solid teaching and experiences that prepared them for a better future. Today the school's mission is still focused on nurturing students, academically and personally, with the help of devoted people who see qualities in them which they cannot yet see in themselves.

I'm now retired and spend a good part of my time on the golf course. My experiences coaching at White's and watching those four young men turn into state champions are among the most treasured memories of my life.

I had the honor of being inducted into the Grant County Sports Hall of Fame on April 15, 2012, which was a culmination of my experiences both as an athlete and a coach. I deeply appreciated the honor and the chance to reconnect with that part of my story.

But the thing no one tells us when we're young is that we don't have to choose between making our mark and investing in relationships. Relationships are the most powerful way to make an indelible impression, on the world *around* us — and the world *inside* us. It is *relationships* that have remained the greatest outcome of those years. Being an athlete and a coach was always about something far more lasting than winning.

Some people may have thought our state championship victory was a fluke or luck. But those of us who were there know better. Our win, against all odds, was the kind of miracle that happens when a group of very imperfect people are courageous enough to believe in something - and Someone - bigger than ourselves, and who keep believing all things are possible if we can just get out of our own way. To me, that 1973 State Championship banner will forever represent our own special miracle at the Tute.

About the Author

A hometown hero from Fairmount, Ind., Chuck "Poke" Gaither is a Grant County Sports Hall of Fame inductee, devoted husband, father, mentor, and now author. Chuck's athletic career is the stuff local legends are made of and his contributions as a coach and mentor have begun a ripple effect in the lives of students that will undoubtedly continue for generations. After retiring from teaching and coaching, Chuck traveled on the crew for the Grammy-winning Gaither Vocal Band for more than a decade.

Chuck and his wife, Becky, have been married for more than 60 years. Becky, too, invested her life in teaching and mentoring students after graduating from Ball State with honors. The Gaithers' oldest daughters, Tammy and Rae-Lee, both became registered nurses. The couple lost Tammy tragically in 1985. Rae is now an advocate for women in prison on death row. Their youngest daughter, Brandi, is a school psychologist and played an instrumental role in turning *"Miracle at the Tute"* into a reality.

Chuck's story, *Miracle at the Tute,* is a heartwarming, true-life tale that reminds us all that miracles happen every day when we are willing to keep showing up, doing the right thing, and caring for the people in our path.

www.ingramcontent.com/pod-product-compliance
Lightning Source LLC
LaVergne TN
LVHW031541060526
838200LV00056B/4594